# A Tunes

## Capricious Pieces for Beginner Violinists

### Elaine Fine

© 2021 by Mel Bay Publications, Inc. All Rights Reserved.
*WWW.MELBAY.COM*

# Introduction

I wrote this set of violin caprices for use by teachers who prefer to introduce note reading simultaneously with beginning violin technique. In musical and lyrical ways, these tuneful solo pieces address some of the technical difficulties encountered in the first few volumes of the popular Suzuki violin books.

The technical challenges herein are presented in the same order that they appear in the Suzuki books. A teacher can use these pieces as preparation for working on a particular Suzuki piece, for technical reinforcement of a skill, or as pieces for solo performance without the need for piano accompaniment.

I introduce slurs early in the book because I believe that the possibilities for expression increase dramatically when a student has the opportunity to experiment with bow speed and bow division. "Starry Night," which uses the pitches found in "Twinkle, Twinkle Little Star," introduces dynamics. In "Wait! What?" the student encounters quarter and half-note rests as well as dynamics. "Breeze in the Trees," a study in arpeggios that incorporates rests and dynamics, will help the student with some of the difficulties in "Song of the Wind."

"The Big Dipper" is simply "Starry Night" set in 3/4 time, but already incorporates slurs. "Solo Two-Step" helps the student feel the half steps between fingers 1 and 2 on the upper two strings, and fingers 3 and 4 on the lower two strings. The slurred version shows the student how different a piece of music can sound and feel with changes in articulation and dynamics.

"String Crossing Waltz" helps students learn to vary the amount and speed of the bow, "Leading-Tone Gallop" strengthens the fourth finger, and "Farmer's Crossing" prepares the student for the bowing difficulties found in "The Happy Farmer." "Gotcha!" will further strengthen the fourth finger, and "Te Unim" isolates and explores the many difficulties found in Beethoven's "Minuet in G."

This book includes a few pieces that have no equivalent in the Suzuki books; for example, "Goodnight Air" is a lesson in rhythm, written with the objective of helping students understand the difference between duplet and triplet eighth notes, as well as the way that meter works. The rhythms come from the text of a well-known bedtime story book and will help the student realize some of the ways that phrasing in music is similar to phrasing in speech or poetry.

"Lullaby for Castor and Pollux" harmonizes the "Starry Night" theme with simple double-stops, and the compound-time dance that follows uses the exact same pitches and rhythms—but has a different meter. "Vocalise" was written to allow the student to feel as if he or she is singing through the violin, and "Appogiare with Variations," which introduces suspensions and combinations of textures, is meant to reinforce the expressive use of the bow through leaning into ascending and descending half steps.

I hope your students enjoy learning these pieces and conquering the challenges they present.

*Elaine Fine*

# Contents

| Title | Page |
|---|---|
| Starry Night | 4 |
| Wait! What? | 5 |
| Breeze in the Trees | 6 |
| The Big Dipper | 7 |
| Solo Two-Step | 8 |
| Slurry Two-Step | 9 |
| String-Crossing Waltz | 10 |
| Leading-Tone Gallop | 11 |
| Slurry Leading-Tone Gallop | 12 |
| Farmer's Crossing | 13 |
| Gotcha! | 14 |
| Goodnight Air | 15 |
| The Fourth Heroic Music | 16 |
| Rest Stop Gavotte | 17 |
| Non-Stop Gavotte | 18 |
| Lullaby for Castor and Pollux | 19 |
| Te Unim | 20 |
| Castor and Pollux Dance | 22 |
| Vocalise | 23 |
| Appogiare with Variations | 24 |

# Starry Night

Elaine Fine

# Wait! What?

Make sure to count one beat during the quarter note rests and two beats during the half note rests.
We don't actually rest during rests--we count silent beats.
Notice that the E in measure 19 is tied to the E in measure 20.

# Breeze in the Trees
## A Trumpet Tune

# The Big Dipper
(A Slurry Starry Night)

# Solo Two-Step

Try your best to feel the closeness of the half-steps between the first and second fingers on the A and E strings, and the closeness of the half-steps between second and third fingers on the D and G strings. When you cross strings in measures 5 and 6, and in measures 17 and 18, try to feel the half-steps between the fingers there as well.

# Slurry Two-Step

Music is so much more than simply pitches and rhythms! The pitches and rhythms here are the same as the previous piece, but playing with slurs and dynamics makes the music feel and sound different.

# String-Crossing Waltz

Use the full bow for the down-bow quarter note, and divide the bow in two parts for the two up-bow quarter notes. Make sure that all the quarter notes last for the same amount of time. Make sure to feel the half steps between the first and second fingers on the A string and second and third fingers on the D string, and observe the two-note slurs.

# Leading-Tone Gallop

The high third finger D sharp is a leading tone that leads to a fourth finger E. Try it slowly at first, and then try it quickly.

# Slurry Leading-Tone Gallop

Now with slurs and dynamics! Try it quickly! Try it slowly!

# Farmer's Crossing
for happier farmers

FOLLOWING THE BOWINGS WILL TEACH YOUR ARM TO CROSS STRINGS UNDER DIFFICULT CIRCUMSTANCES. DON'T FORGET TO FEEL THE HALF STEPS BETWEEN THE FIRST AND SECOND FINGERS ON THE UPPER TWO STRINGS. KEEP THE THIRD FINGER ON BOTH STRINGS IN MEASURES 22 AND 23.

# Gotcha!

# Goodnight Air

**Very calm and relaxed**

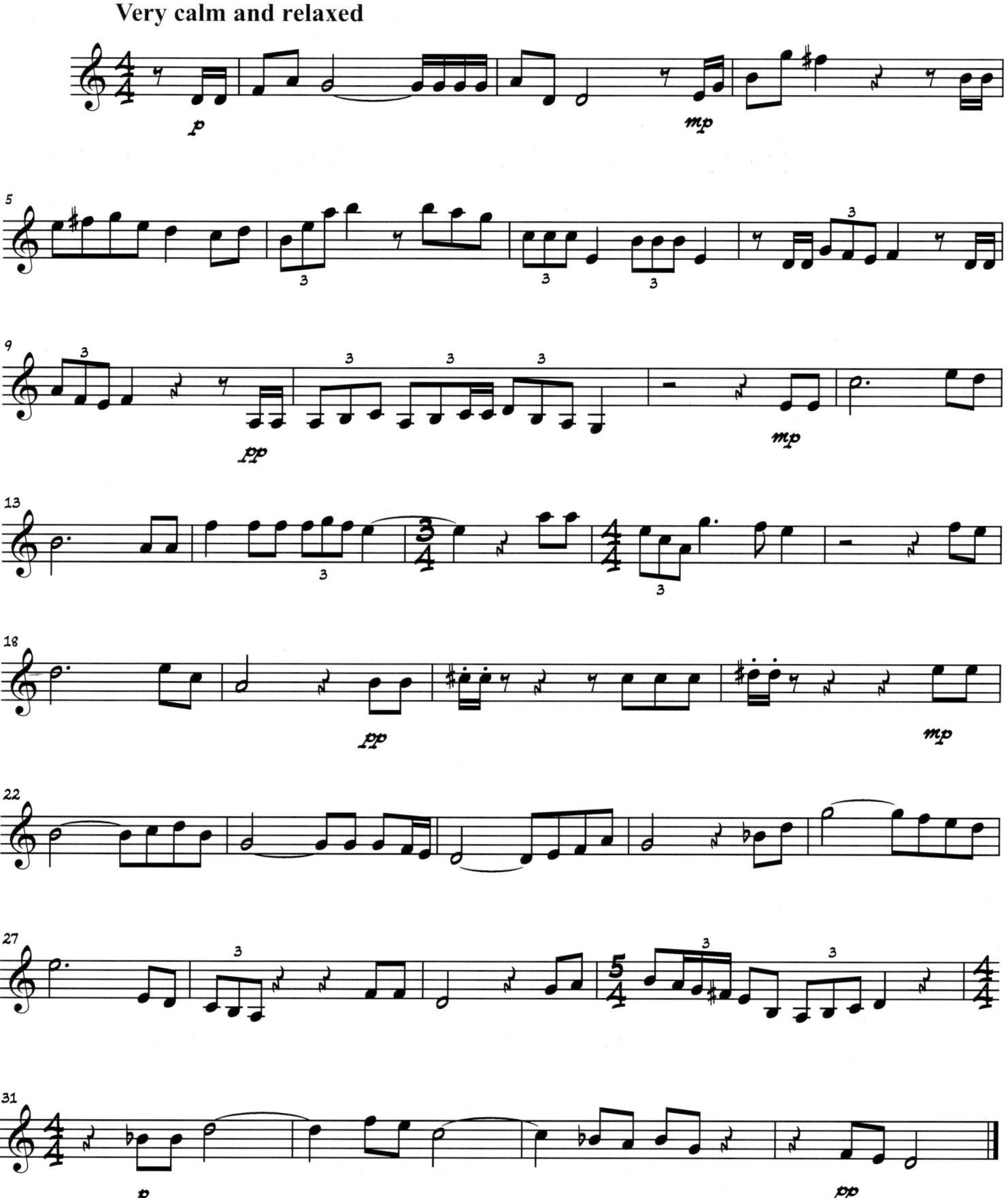

# The Fourth Heroic Muse

May the fourth (finger) be with you.

# Rest Stop Gavotte

Keep the bow on the string during the rests. That way you can get the fingers of the left hand ready for what follows.

# Non-Stop Gavotte

See if you can mentally prepare the left hand while the bow is moving!

# Lullaby for Castor and Pollux

(A two-voice variation on Starry Night)

# Te Unim

"Te unim" means "We unite you" in Romanian, and in Hebrew it means to toil. But it is also the backwards spelling of Minuet. Practicing this should help you navigate the chromatic half-position waters of the Beethoven Minuet in G.

# Castor and Pollux Dance
(A compound-time dance version of the Lullaby)

THE PITCHES AND RHYTHMS ARE EXACTLY THE SAME AS IN THE LULLABY, BUT WITH THE COMPOUND-TIME METER, THE LIVELY TEMPO, AND THE LOUDER DYNAMIC MARKING, THE MUSIC SOUNDS QUITE DIFFERENT!

# Vocalise

**Lentamente, molto cantabile**

# Appogiare with Variations

# Other Mel Bay Violin Books

Beginner Violin Theory for Children Book One (M. Smith)
Beginner Violin Theory for Children Book Two (M. Smith)
Complete Violin Scale Dictionary (Isaac)
Daily Scale Exercises for Violin (Chang)
Essential Scales and Studies for Violin, Level 1 (C. Duncan)
Finger Fun: A Workbook for First Position Violin (Silberman)
Finger Positions for the Violin (Gilland)
Forty Studies for Violin (Chang)
Gypsy Violin (Harbar)
Mandolin for Violinists (Driscoll)
Past the Print (Waller)
Plugging In: A Guide to Gear and New Techniques for the 21st Century Violinist (Deninzon)
Practice for Performance for Violin (DeForest)
Progressive Scale Studies for Violin (Bauer)
Sensible Scales Plus! (Waller)
Speed-Reading for Violin (Bauer)
Technical Studies for Beginning Violin (C. Duncan)
The Student Violinist's Guide to Music Theory (Swoveland)
The Violin/Fiddle Manual and Encyclopedia of Techniques: How to do Anything on the Instrument (Willis)
Third Position Easy & Melodic Violin Etudes (Swoveland)
Violin Wall Chart (Norgaard)
Warm-Ups for the Violinist (Wheeler)
Beginning Violinist's Songbook (Maroni)
Easy Classics for Violin with Piano Accompaniment (Spitzer)
Easy Solos for Beginning Violin Level 1 (C. Duncan)
Easy Solos for Violin (Bluestone)
Easy Way Christmas Song Folio: C Instruments (W. Bay)
Fun with the Violin (W. Bay)
Great Fiddling Tunes - Fun Solos to Play (C. Duncan)
Lively Violin Tunes (W. Bay)
More Fun with the Violin (W. Bay)
My Very Best Christmas Violin (Khanagov)
Solo Pieces for the Beginning Violinist (C. Duncan)
Solo Pieces for the Intermediate Violinist (C. Duncan)
The Student Violinist: Bach (C. Duncan)
The Student Violinist: Beethoven (C. Duncan)
The Student Violinist: Brahms (C. Duncan)
The Student Violinist: Handel (C. Duncan)

**WWW.MELBAY.COM**

# Mel Bay Violin Duet and Ensemble Books

American Fiddle Tunes for Solo and Ensemble: Violin 1 and 2 (C. Duncan)

Celtic Fiddle Tunes for Solo and Ensemble: Violin 1 and 2 (C. Duncan)

Christmas Music Arranged for Violin Duet (Staidle)

Christmas Strings: Violin 1 & 2 with Piano Accompaniment (Miller)

Come Fiddle with Me (Hay)

Come Fiddle with Me Volume Two (Hay)

Eastern European Music for Violin Duet (Harbar)

Easy Classics for Violin with Piano Accompaniment (Spitzer)

Easy Duets for Violin (Puscoiu)

Easy Violin Duets in First Position (Isaac)

Fiddling Classics for Solo and Ensemble: Violins 1 and 2 (C. Duncan)

J. S. Bach: Duets for Two Violins (Spencer/Engle)

Jazz Duets: Violin Edition (Biondi)

Music from Around the World for Solo and Ensemble: Violin 1 & 2 (Miller)

Ragtimes for Two Violins (Brydern)

Scottish Airs and Dances for Violin Solo or Duet (Witt)

Scottish Melodies for Violin Solo or Duet (Witt)

Twin Fiddling (Phillips)

Violin Duet Classics Made Playable (Harbar)

Wedding Music for String Quartet (Staidle)

Wedding Music for Two Violins (Staidle)

WWW.MELBAY.COM